Go-Kart Surprise

written by Lucinda Cotter

illustrated by Gaston Vanzet

"How many times do I have to tell you!" said Mick, patting his little brother on the head.
"You're too little to race."

Justin gave Mick his crash helmet
and gloves.
"But it's my birthday next week," he said,
"and I'll be eight.
I can start racing when I'm eight."

Mick just smiled as he put
on his helmet and gloves.
Then he jumped into his go-kart
and *z o o m e d* off for a practice lap.

"Mick gets to have all the fun," thought Justin.

"All I do is watch **him** and help out." Justin kicked at some stones on the ground, as he slowly walked over to Mum.

"Hello," said Mum.
"It's almost race time.
How do you think Mick will do today?"

Justin didn't say anything.

"You're very quiet," said Mum.
"Is everything okay?"

"I want to race, too," he said sadly.

Mum patted him on the back.
"You can race when you're a bit older," she said.

Just then, the green light went on and the race started.

"Go Mick!" shouted Mum.

The go-karts *z o o m e d* past with a roar.

Justin watched as the go-karts
sped round the track.
A bright red go-kart with black stripes
was in first place.
As the red go-kart went
around the last corner,
Mick roared past it.
Mick had won the race!

"Well done!" yelled Mum from the side.

"I could do that," thought Justin.
"I could be a great go-kart driver, too."

At dinner, Mum smiled at Mick as she placed some more chicken on his plate.
"That was a really great race today," she said.

"Thanks, Mum," said Mick, smiling back at her.

Justin wasn't hungry at all.
"Why did Mick have to come first?"
he thought.
"And why did he have to put his trophy on the dinner table.
Everything is **always** about Mick."

The next Saturday was Justin's birthday.
Three of his best friends came to his party.
Mum had bought pizza
and made a chocolate cake.
Justin should have been having fun,
but he wasn't.

Mum came out with her car keys.
"Come on, everyone," she smiled.
"We are all going for a ride in the van."

"Where are we going?" asked Justin.

Mum just smiled.

It didn't take long before Justin knew where they were going. Mum was taking them to the go-kart track!

When they arrived, Mick was there with some of his friends. There were four go-karts waiting on the track.

"Yippee!" cried Justin, running over to Mick. "I can race today."

Mick smiled.
"You have to put on your safety gear first," he said.

Once everyone was in their safety gear,
and had gone over the rules,
they were ready to race.

Mick showed Justin a go-kart
with the number 8 on it.
"Happy birthday, little brother,"
he laughed.
"It's race time!"